Survival

Although people can live for a long time, sometimes as long as several weeks, without food, they can only live for a few days without drinking. Living cells are made up of protoplasm, which is mainly water, and so all living things need water.

As so many things will dissolve in water, it is very suitable for carrying chemicals inside living things. In people, for instance, food which has been digested is carried around the body in the blood. The blood also carries oxygen from the air in the lungs to the muscles, and it carries waste away from the muscles to the lungs and kidneys. Water acts as a transport system for plants as well as for animals.

Drinking water

Most water, even tap water, has many different chemicals dissolved in it. Some of these chemicals are picked up as the rain water runs through rocks and soil. Water which is to be piped to houses has other chemicals added to it. Chlorine is one of these. It is added because it kills bacteria and makes the water safe to drink.

Water is not always a liquid. When it boils, it becomes steam which can be carried away by the air. When it is very cold, water freezes and becomes ice.

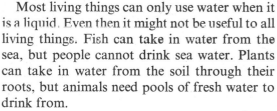

▲
Plants growing by the waterside. Green plants grow best where they have plenty of light and water

Most living things can only use water when it is a liquid. Even then it might not be useful to all living things. Fish can take in water from the sea, but people cannot drink sea water. Plants can take in water from the soil through their roots, but animals need pools of fresh water to drink from.

Dehydration

The food that animals eat is usually mostly water. When we buy fruit and vegetables about 90 per cent of what we are getting is water!

If all the water is removed from food such as fruit, meat, or vegetable, it is reduced in both size and weight. For this reason, dried out, or *dehydrated*, vegetables and meat are easier to store and transport than fresh food. Dehydration also preserves food.

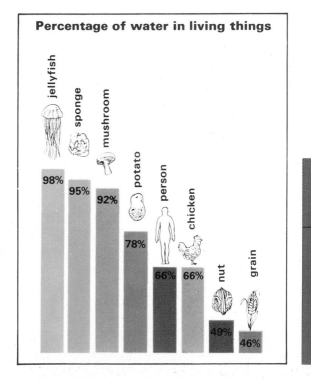

Percentage of water in living things

jellyfish	sponge	mushroom	potato	person	chicken	nut	grain
98%	95%	92%	78%	66%	66%	49%	46%

Percentage of water in human tissue	
Blood	80%
Bone	25%
Liver	70%
Muscle	75%
Skin	70%

1. If a man weighs 65 kilos, what would he weigh if all the water in his body were removed?
2. When you buy 3 kilos of potatoes, how much of that is water?
3. Find out about four of the substances which are dissolved in tap water.
4. Think of ways you could get fresh water from sea water using ordinary household equipment.

1

The sun warms the surface of the water

The water below the surface is still cold

The surface of the water cools

Warmer water from below rises

▲ Life probably developed in the sea because its temperature is fairly constant. Water takes longer to heat up and to cool down than the air around it. The water warms slowly during hot weather, and when the air around it cools, only the surface is affected. Warmer water from below the surface rises to take its place. The sea is at a more or less constant temperature. So also is the land close to it compared to places far from the sea

Life in the sea in the Paleozoic era, more than four hundred million years ago. These creatures existed two hundred million years before the first land animals appeared. Trilobites had hard shells, and their fossilised remains can still be found in rocks today

sponge

trilobite

Life in the sea

Most scientists believe that life began millions of years ago in the water, and continued to first develop in salty water, rather like our present-day seas. There are several reasons for this.

The temperature of the sea changes so little it would give the earliest primitive forms of life the best chance of surviving. The diagram above shows why the temperature of the sea is fairly constant.

Many chemicals are dissolved in sea water. One of these is salt, which gives sea water its taste. The water in plant and animal cells also contains many dissolved chemicals, and is more like sea water than fresh water. The first living things would need the chemicals from sea water, and could get them most easily if they lived there.

Many of the plants and animals which live in water are supported by the water. Seaweed is one of these. It stands up in the water but flops over as soon as it is taken out. The first plants and animals had no skeletons to support them.

Things appear to weigh less in water. For instance, one person can support the entire weight of another, using only one hand, if the person being lifted is in water.

Photosynthesis in water plants

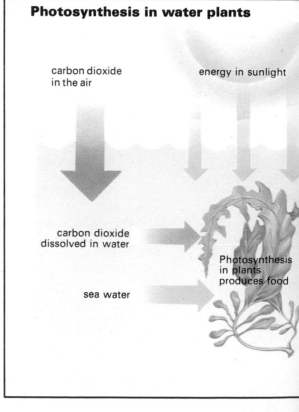

carbon dioxide in the air

energy in sunlight

carbon dioxide dissolved in water

sea water

Photosynthesis in plants produces food

jellyfish

1. Why is it likely that early forms of life developed in the sea?
2. Take a drop of pond water and look at it under a microscope. Describe what you see.
3. What are the two most important substances that plants provide for animals?
4. Why do you think that so few animals and plants are found at very great depths in the sea?
5. Contrary to popular belief, sharks do not feed exclusively on people. Find out what two different kinds of shark eat.
6. Winters in the west coast of Scotland, near the sea, are much milder than winters in Moscow, which is far from the sea. Why do you think that this should be so?

whale

shark

jellyfish

squid

sea horse

Animals adapt to suit their surroundings, but they do this in many different ways. The whale for instance, uses the water to support its enormous weight (the sperm whale in this picture could weigh as much as 60 tonnes), while the jellyfish and the sea horse need the water to support their fragile bodies. The shark, like many other fishes, has a streamlined shape for fast swimming

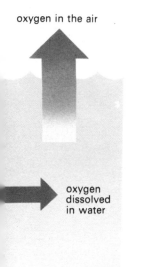

oxygen in the air

oxygen dissolved in water

Simple plants

Animals eat plants, or they eat other animals which eat plants. If there were no plants there would be no animals either, so it seems likely that the first forms of life must have been plants.

The first plants were very simple. They were made up of one cell, which contained *chlorophyll*. Carbon dioxide, as well as the other chemicals that the first plants needed for food, was all around them, dissolved in the sea water

Simple, single-celled plants still exist. The alga chlorella is one of these. Although plants of this sort have changed or evolved since they were first formed, they show that this sort of plant can survive.

Plants evolved from their original simple form, and became larger. When they are made up of many cells, they are called *multicellular*.

Photosynthesis

Water plants, like other plants, make their own food by *photosynthesis*. During this process, the plants use the sun's energy to produce oxygen from carbon dioxide. At first, the oxygen dissolves in the water surrounding the plant. Later, it enters the air. All the oxygen we breathe comes from plants and much of it comes from the simplest of them, the one-celled plants which float in water.

Animals in the sea

The animals which live in the sea today have changed or *evolved* in ways which would not have been possible had they not had the water to support them. Some, like the sea horse, have become very delicate, while others, such as the giant squid, are very large.

Some kinds of whale are about the largest animals which have ever existed. If a whale is stranded out of the water it will soon die, because its skeleton is not strong enough to support the weight of its body, and the whale is crushed to death. But it can live in water, because the water gives it support.

The streamlined shape of the shark is perfect for swimming very fast. The powerful tail pushes the shark's body along, while the fins are used for steering, and as brakes and stabilisers.

Other fish have the same powerful tail movements. Some, like the salmon as it leaps, can push themselves right out of the water. The flying-fish can glide above the surface for many metres.

Some sea animals have evolved in such a way that they hardly need to move at all. The sea anemone is one of these. It stays in one place, fastened to a rock in a pool and waits for the tide to wash over it, carrying small living creatures. The anemone catches these with its tentacles.

The success of plants

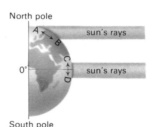

A fossil plant. Ferns existed millions of years before the first flowering plants appeared

There are fossils in rocks which are almost 500 million years old. Since that time the land and the plants growing there have changed, and they are still changing today.

Land plants, unlike sea plants which live surrounded by food and water, have had to adapt in all sorts of ways to the task of finding food and water in many different conditions. The ways in which they have adapted depends on the plants' surroundings.

Plant life is affected by the temperatures of the place in which it grows, by the amount of rain it gets, by the soil in which it grows, and by the rocks beneath the soil.

The map shows the different areas in which plants grow. Mountains, the amount of rainfall, changes in temperature, the distance from the sea a place is, are all things that affect the kind of plants that grow in each area.

The kind of land on which the plants are growing also makes a difference. Water will run through limestone, for example, but not through clay. The types of plants growing in these two soils are often different.

Snow and tundra

Around the North and South poles are areas of permanent snow, where plants cannot grow at all. Next to this permanent snow area is a land called the *tundra* which has a brief summer.

Plants cannot live in very cold places where the water is always frozen. Where the snow melts for a short time, it may make just enough water for plants like moss, lichens, short tough grass and dwarf shrubs to grow.

However much water there is in the soil, it is useless if it is frozen solid. This is the case above the snow line on high mountains. Plant life just below the snow line on mountains is very like that of the tundra.

Coniferous forest

Coniferous trees are those, like pine trees, which produce cones to carry their seeds. Conifers grow in places which have warm summers and cold winters. Most have thin, pointed leaves called needles. These are particularly suitable for the climate in which the trees grow. During a cold winter water may be frozen and the air becomes dry. The moisture in ordinary leaves would soon evaporate away, but the needles of a conifer hardly lose any water.

Deciduous forest and grassland

Most deciduous trees lose all their leaves in winter. The tree then needs less water and is less likely to be damaged by frost than a tree that keeps all its leaves.

A few deciduous trees do not lose all their

Near the equator (C to D), the sun's rays are concentrated making the surface of the earth much warmer than at the poles (A to B). Plant life, however, is not only affected by how near to the equator it lives. The altitude, the soil on which plants grow and the amount of rainfall in an area all go towards making the different kinds of plant life in different parts of the world. On this map, savannah has been included with deciduous forest and grassland

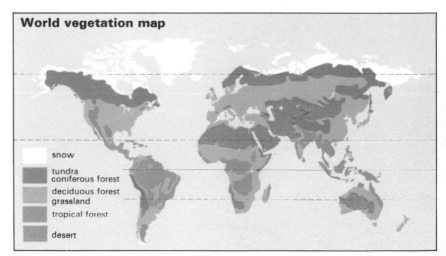

World vegetation map

snow

tundra
coniferous forest

deciduous forest
grassland

tropical forest

desert

leaves. Rhododendrons and laurels are among these, as well as evergreen oaks. Their leaves are especially tough and are protected by a wax-like coating.

Most of Europe and North America are in the region where deciduous forests used to grow. Much of this land is now grassland.

Tropical rain forest
Tropical rain forests grow near the equator, where the sun is hot and there is plenty of rain. The trees grow so close together that their leaves form a cover which stops the land from drying out in spite of the heat from the sun. The air beneath the trees stays very moist.

Savannah and desert
If the rainfall in an area is very low, the land is covered with bush, scrub and grass. This kind of land is called savannah. The game parks of Africa are an example of savannah. Savannah is not as valuable to farmers as grassland, though it can be used for sheep and cattle ranches. Deserts support very little life.

Agriculture and water
In many parts of the world plants cannot easily grow because there is a lack of water. So people must pipe it to their land or even alter the course of rivers. Sometimes they build dams to store the water until they need it.

Primitive methods of irrigation in Algeria help farmers to grow crops in an area where the rainfall is very low

Grasslands are ideal areas for grain farming, as this picture of wheat farming on the Canadian prairie shows

Taking water to plants in this way is called *irrigation*. It has been done in places like Egypt and China for thousands of years. In Australia today, people are using irrigation to try to make plants grow in some of the driest desert country in the world. Much more land could also be used for crops, but such irrigation is expensive.

Plants that have returned to water
Some plants evolved to be land plants but then returned to live in the water. Water lilies are an example of this. They grow with their roots in the soil at the bottom of a pond and with their large leaves floating on the surface.

1. Reindeer live in the tundra. What sort of plants do you think they eat?
2. Why are there not many plants growing under the trees in tropical rain forests where there is plenty of water?
3. Britain is as far north as Labrador, but the vegetation is quite different. How do you account for this?

5

Water and reproduction

The amoeba is a single-clled animal which lives in water. It reproduces by splitting in two, as shown in the diagram. The two parts of the amoeba move off separately. This kind of reproduction is called asexual

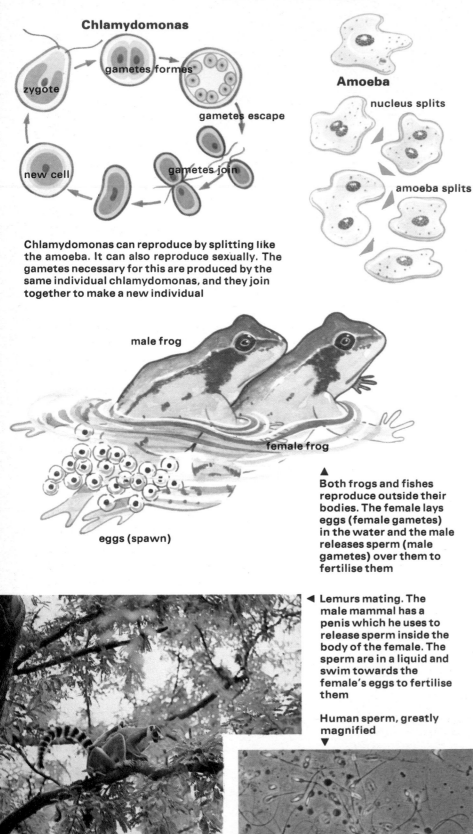

Chlamydomonas

gametes formes*

zygote

gametes escape

new cell

gametes join

Chlamydomonas can reproduce by splitting like the amoeba. It can also reproduce sexually. The gametes necessary for this are produced by the same individual chlamydomonas, and they join together to make a new individual

Amoeba

nucleus splits

amoeba splits

male frog

female frog

eggs (spawn)

▲ Both frogs and fishes reproduce outside their bodies. The female lays eggs (female gametes) in the water and the male releases sperm (male gametes) over them to fertilise them

◀ Lemurs mating. The male mammal has a penis which he uses to release sperm inside the body of the female. The sperm are in a liquid and swim towards the female's eggs to fertilise them

Human sperm, greatly magnified
▼

Both plants and animals need water to reproduce.

The simplest living things, like the amoeba, reproduce by splitting in two. More complicated plants and animals reproduce *sexually*. This means that reproduction involves the production of two cells called *gametes*, which join together to make a new individual.

Animals, such as fish and frogs, which mate in water, use the water to bring the male and female eggs together. The eggs are fertilised when a male gamete joins with a female one. The water keeps the fertilised eggs at an even temperature and provides them with oxygen. It also removes waste.

Land animals

Animals which mate on land have to provide a liquid for the male gametes to swim in as they make their way to the female gametes. This liquid is produced in the body of the male. It is passed into the body of the female during mating.

Birds' eggs are fertilised and then encased in a hard shell before they are laid. The shell is important as it stops the egg from drying out.

A mammal's eggs are also fertilised in the body of the female. The egg then remains inside her body, enclosed in a bag of protective fluid until the young mammal is ready to emerge. Also see 'Reproduction and growth'.

Plants

Mosses, ferns and many other plants cannot be fertilised unless they have at least a thin covering of water for the gametes to swim in.

Flowering plants do not need water in this way. They reproduce by making *pollen*, which is little grains containing the male gametes.

Once the pollen has reached the female part of the flower it produces a tube, which grows towards the *ovule* (egg), which is the female gamete. This tube will only grow if there is moisture available, so that even plants which make pollen still need water to reproduce.

1. Frogs sometimes travel long distances from the damp places in which they live to ponds where they mate and lay eggs. Why do you think that there are so many dead frogs on the roads in spring?
2. Find out about the marine turtle and where it lays its eggs.
3. Give one reason why mosses grow best in damp conditions.

Protection from water

Many animals have oil in their coats which prevents them suffering too much from the cold if they get wet. Some animals, such as this polar bear, which spends much of its life in the cold Arctic sea, are especially well designed for this

The caddis fly larva makes a heavy tube to stop fast flowing water from washing it away. The tube also makes good camouflage

1. Several times recently, birds covered in oil have been found on the beach. Various harmless chemicals can be used to remove the oil. If the birds are freed immediately after cleaning they become wet and cold and often die. Can you explain this?
2. Look in a book about the seashore and name two plants and four animals which live between the levels of the high and low tides. Find out how each manages to stay where it is despite the movements of the tides.
3. Give three ways in which small animals can protect themselves from damage and being washed away in fast flowing streams.

Many animals which live in water either permanently or just occasionally enjoy the advantages it brings, but they have to develop special means of overcoming the disadvantages too.

Mammals

Mammals are warm blooded. If their fur became very wet every time it rained, the water would cool them down too much.

If you have been near to a wet dog shaking itself, you will know that it can shake off nearly all the water from its skin. The dog's fur is kept waterproof by the oil produced by special glands. Most mammals have similar oil glands.

Mammals which spend a part of each day in water have especially waterproof coats. These coats do not only keep the animal dry, but while they are in the water, the fur traps a layer of air next to the skin and this keeps the animal warm.

Sea mammals with little or no fur tend to have extra fat or blubber beneath the skin to keep them warm.

Birds

Birds, like mammals, are warm blooded. They need oils to keep their feathers dry, and to keep them warm. Wet feathers would make the bird too heavy to fly. Water birds, such as ducks, have particularly waterproof feathers.

Plants

Many plants try to keep their leaves dry. Some leaves are covered with microscopic hairs which will keep drops of liquid from reaching the surface of a leaf.

Fast moving water

A fresh-water pond is full of all kinds of living things. The water in a pond is fairly still and so can support upright plants, tadpoles which swim about, and even pond skaters which walk about on the surface of the water.

It is difficult for plants to grow in fast flowing water. If there are plants in the water they are usually rooted near the bank. They may trail out into the faster flowing part of the water.

Some small animals fasten themselves to stones so that they can stay in one place in a fast flowing stream. Others, such as the caddis fly larva, make a heavy tube of stones to shelter in and to make it difficult for the water to wash them away. Other animals do not hold on to anything. They shelter under rocks, waiting for the water to wash food towards them. For more about this, see 'Urban ecology', in this series.

Water and seeds

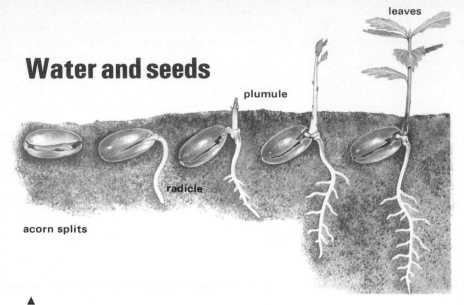

leaves

plumule

radicle

acorn splits

▲ An acorn begins to grow. It swells, breaks its case and then puts down its first root, or radicle. This is followed by a shoot which appears above the ground. Once green leaves are formed the plant can make its food by photosynthesis

Rice growing. Rice needs plenty of water and is grown in countries where there is a heavy rainfall at the right time of year. The nutrients the young plants need come from organic waste previously spread on the land

Plants need water before they can even begin to grow from seeds.

A seed has a thick protective coat, which surrounds a food store and an *embryo* which will grow into a new plant. When a seed is sown it will not germinate unless water enters it. Chemicals called enzymes use the water to break down the food store so that it can be carried to the embryo.

The first part of the embryo to grow out from the seed is called the *radicle*. This acts as a root taking in more water. The *plumule*, which will form all the parts of the plant to appear above ground, can then use the remaining food store to give it the energy it needs to grow up through the soil.

Once above the ground, a plant can make its own food by photosynthesis. It obtains the water and the mineral salts it needs from the soil, and so thrives best on damp fertile land.

Flooding

This is particularly important in a country like Bangladesh, which is often very wet indeed. The area is prone to much dangerous flooding which can cause enormous damage. But the ground there is very fertile, as the flood water which covers it so often carries valuable minerals with it.

As a swollen river rushes along, the stones it takes with it crash into each other, and gradually break down. This process makes deep valleys at first, and produces soil which is left behind as the river spreads on to flatter ground. In areas prone to flooding, new fertile soil is swept over the land every year and left behind by the flood.

Erosion

Plants grow best on a hillside if there are other plants, with large roots, keeping the soil in one place. Where people have removed natural vegetation, rain water, far from helping young plants to grow, simply washes the fertile soil off the hillside, leaving barren rock. This is called *soil erosion.*

1. The Nile delta used to flood annually. Why did the farmers of Ancient Egypt need to be good surveyors?
2. How are farmers in the Far East able to grow rice, which needs so much water, on steep hillsides?
3. There are ways that new young plants will grow other than from seed. Find out what these are.

Flooding in Bangladesh. There are areas of the world which are prone to heavy floods. Although they provide good conditions for farming, they can also cause a lot of damage with many thousands of deaths

Roots

Although water will normally only flow downhill, it must travel upwards through the stem of a plant to reach the leaves and flowers.

Water can be made to move upwards if it is pumped, or if it is put under some sort of pressure. A spring bubbles up from under the ground because it has been forced up by some pressure below the surface of the ground.

Water can also be sucked upwards. This is what happens when a person drinks through a straw. Plants use their leaves to draw water from the ground in this way, and suck it through their stems from the roots.

Most plants are anchored by roots. These may go deep into the ground, or they may spread out broadly just below the surface of the ground.

Root tips

The tips of the roots of a plant are covered with fine white hairs. These root hairs grow out between soil particles and take up water and mineral salts. If the root hairs are damaged, the plant cannot get enough water and may die.

This explains why a plant which had been dug up and replanted may die even though it seems to have plenty of roots. The roots left on the

root hairs

The tip of a root

plant may only be the ones which are used to anchor it. The tips of the roots, which take up the water the plant needs, may be damaged and useless.

Osmosis

Water tends to move from a weak solution to a strong one. When this happens in a situation where there is a living barrier of *protoplasm*, water can pass through the barrier to reach the strong solution but the chemicals in the strong solution cannot escape. The protoplasm thus acts like a sieve and so is called a *semi-permeable membrane*. This process is called *osmosis*. Root hairs draw moisture from the soil by osmosis.

Sugar beet, for example, contains a strong solution of sugar in its roots. It can take a lot of water from the soil. Most plants have less sugar in them, but they usually have enough chemicals in their roots to attract water into the plant.

If a lawn has too much fertiliser on it, it turns brown and dies. This is because the chemicals in the fertiliser make the water in the soil into a solution which is stronger than the solution of chemicals in the lawn grass. So water cannot pass into the grass by osmosis, but stays in the ground instead. Some water may even leave the grass to join the strong solution in the soil. The grass dries out and dies.

1. Look at the osmosis experiment on the right. What do you think would happen if you put water in the hollowed out potato and sugar in the dish?
2. Why do you think that plants growing in mud flats have so much in common with plants growing in dry places?
3. Explain why potato chips become slightly longer when they are left in water for some time
4. In winter, salt is sometimes put on the roads. Find out why this happens. Why does the salt kill some of the roadside plants?

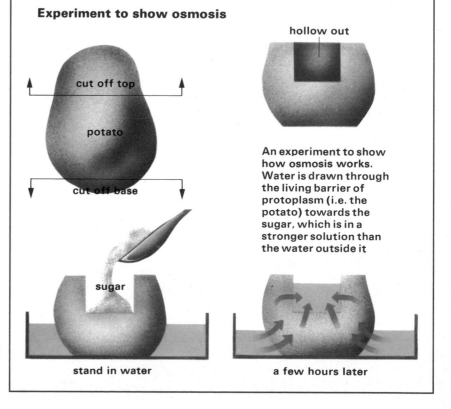

Experiment to show osmosis

cut off top

potato

cut off base

sugar

stand in water

hollow out

An experiment to show how osmosis works. Water is drawn through the living barrier of protoplasm (i.e. the potato) towards the sugar, which is in a stronger solution than the water outside it

a few hours later

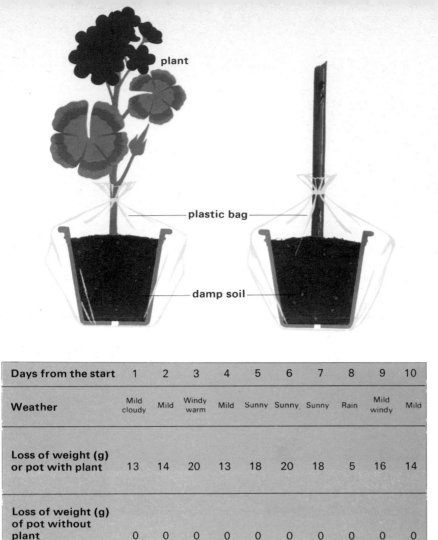

plant

plastic bag

damp soil

Days from the start	1	2	3	4	5	6	7	8	9	10
Weather	Mild cloudy	Mild	Windy warm	Mild	Sunny	Sunny	Sunny	Rain	Mild windy	Mild
Loss of weight (g) or pot with plant	13	14	20	13	18	20	18	5	16	14
Loss of weight (g) of pot without plant	0	0	0	0	0	0	0	0	0	0

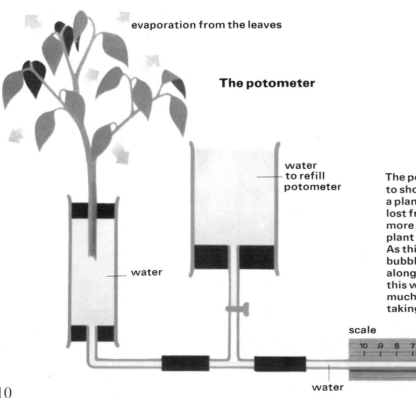

evaporation from the leaves

The potometer

water to refill potometer

water

water

scale

air bubble

Leaves

Plants take water from the soil and lose it through their leaves. The experiment on the left explains how this can be measured by comparing the weight of a pot with a plant with the weight of a pot with a stick over a period of time.

The experiment also shows how different kinds of weather affect the speed at which plants take water from the soil. The sort of very dry or dry and windy weather which is best for drying clothes is also the sort of weather that dries plants out.

Anyone who keeps indoor plants will know just how often they need watering. Different plants need different amounts of water. A plant which does not get enough water will wilt and die. Too much water can also kill the plant because it can make its roots rot.

The potometer
Scientists have accurate methods which they use to work out how much water a plant will take from the soil. One of these involves a piece of apparatus called a *potometer*.

If just one branch of a plant, for example, a cotton plant is tested, a scientist can work out how much water the whole plant needs. Experiments like these are very important to farmers, who have to know exactly how much water their crops need.

In areas where water is scarce, farmers cannot afford to waste it. They need to know exactly how much water to pump through their irrigation ditches so that, on the one hand, none of it runs away and is wasted. On the other hand, if the plants do not get enough water, they will dry out and die.

The potometer is used to show how much water a plant uses. As water is lost from the leaves, more is drawn into the plant through the stem. As this happens, the bubble of air is drawn along the scale, and in this way it shows how much water the plant is taking up

1. Young plants are often put in pots until they have grown strong enough to be planted outside in the open. Why do you think that the plants stand the best chance of survival if the pot containing them is placed inside a clear polythene bag?

The structure of a leaf

Leaves are covered with a wax-like layer called the *cuticle*. The cuticle is waterproof. The layer of cells which surround the leaf and make the cuticle is called the *epidermis*. The cells of the epidermis fit closely together, and this, as well as the cuticle make it difficult for water to escape.

Water can still evaporate from the leaves. It escapes through small holes called the *stomata*. Each stomata is opened and closed by two sausage-shaped *guard cells*. The stomata open to let in carbon dioxide which the plant needs to make food for itself. When the guard cells are open, a little water vapour escapes from the leaves. This is called *transpiration*.

Inside a leaf

Light versus transpiration

A plant has to have large enough leaves to catch as much light as it needs to make plenty of food for itself. The larger the area of leaf, however, the more water evaporates through transpiration.

Some plants, such as tomatoes, have very large leaves. These help them to make plenty of food, but they also lose a lot of water through transpiration. The plants wilt very quickly and in a hot summer tomato growers have to water their plants several times a day.

Plants which grow under the canopy of trees in a tropical rain forest can afford to grow large leaves. They need these to gain light in the shady forest. The plant does not dry out because the trees above protect it from the sun.

Tobacco plants

Tobacco growers use the same idea when they are growing the very large tobacco leaves they need to wrap cigars in.

The tobacco leaves must be large enough and thin enough to roll easily. They are grown under sheets of thin cotton, which, like the canopy of leaves in a rain forest, allows the leaves to grow large without drying out too much.

Some gardeners spread muslin over their crop for the same reasons. Painting whitewash over a greenhouse has the same effect, and helps to stops the plants from drying out.

1. What sort of weather makes a plant wilt?
2. Why do you think that the holly and other evergreens have a very thick cuticle?
3. Why do you think that shrubs can be dug up and moved to new ground in autumn, but if they are moved to new ground in summer they often die?

▲ A bird's nest fern in a tropical rain forest in Madagascar. Like many other plants of wet, tropical jungles it has large leaves which can absorb as much light as possible without any danger of drying out

◄ Young tobacco plants in North America are protected from the weather by sheets of muslin

Inside the trunk of a tree

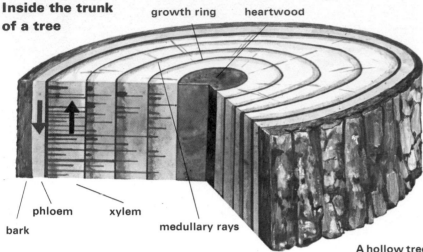

growth ring • heartwood

phloem • xylem

bark

medullary rays

A hollow tree ▶

Wood

Once the water has been sucked into the stem of a plant, it passes along the plant through water-carrying cells which work like drinking straws. A plant can use these cells even without roots. A cut flower, for example can live for several days in a vase of water.

If a drinking straw bends it collapses and is useless. The water-carrying cells in a plant also become useless once they have collapsed. If water cannot rise through the stem to the leaf the plant will die, so the water-carrying cells must have thick, strong walls that do not break easily.

Xylem

In a tree, these water-carrying cells grow close together. They make wood, which is called *xylem*.

A tree forms a new ring of xylem on the outside of the trunk just under the bark, every year. This means that every year the trunk gets a little thicker. If a tree is cut down, you can work out its age by counting the number of rings of xylem.

Some tree trunks are very thick, but trees only carry water up to their leaves through the outer rings of xylem. The older wood in the centre of the trunk is less important. It sometimes rots away, so that the tree becomes hollow.

The phloem runs between the bark and the outside ring of xylem. It transports the food which is made by the leaves to the roots.

Timber

Trees are very useful as timber. When a tree is cut down, the outer wood, the new xylem, is cut off. This outer layer is called the *sapwood*, because it is full of moisture. The inner wood can be used to make buildings and furniture and many other things.

If wood is used to make things as soon as it has been felled, there is a danger that it will start to bend later on. This bending is called *warping*. It happens because even the older wood in a tree contains some moisture, and, as it dries out, the wood changes shape.

The most expensive timber is left to dry for a

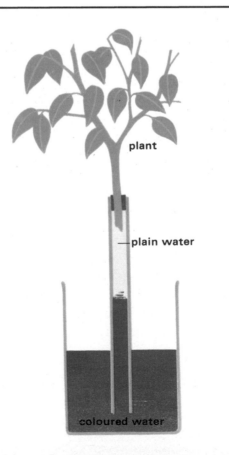

This experiment shows how a plant sucks in water through its stem, even when the roots have been cut off. The dish is full of coloured water. The glass tube in which the plant is fixed is full of clear water at the start of the experiment. It is open at the bottom. Hold a card over the bottom of the tube to stop the clear water running out, and place the tube in the dish of coloured water. Remove the card. You will now have the tube of clear water standing in the dish. As the plant draws water up through its stem, the coloured water will enter the tube and rise up it

plant

plain water

coloured water

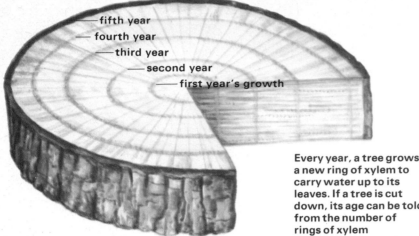

first year's growth
second year
third year
fourth year
fifth year

Every year, a tree grows a new ring of xylem to carry water up to its leaves. If a tree is cut down, its age can be told from the number of rings of xylem

Changes in the weather ▶ and the amount of moisture in the air have made the timbers on this old house warp

long time before it is used, or is dried in kilns. Furniture wood should have just about the same amount of moisture in it as is found in the atmosphere in an ordinary house. This makes sure the wood will not warp.

Some trees, such as pines, form a gummy resin in their trunks. This gum keeps water from seeping into the tree and rotting the wood.

Many Canadian houses are built with a type of pine wood which is so full of gum that it lasts for years without needing to be painted. A similar kind of gum fills the wood of the ebony tree. This helps to make it one of the heaviest woods. Balsa wood has almost no gum in it, and so is very light.

Veneers

Woods like rosewood and teak are so expensive that many people cannot afford to buy furniture made from them. But it is possible to cut wood into very thin sheets. These sheets can be almost as thin as the wood which peels off a pencil when it is turned in a pencil sharpener.

These thin sheets of wood are called *veneers*. They can be stuck over cheap wood or chipboard, to make them look like expensive wood. Veneers are so thin that they contain very little moisture and so they do not warp.

1. The diagram above shows a cross-section of a tree. How old was the tree when it was cut down?
2. What are the ways in which an animal loses water from its body?
3. Find out what sorts of wood are used for veneers.
4. Draw a diagram similar to the water cycle diagram shown, to illustrate the carbon cycle.
5. If you examined the sawn-off stump of a very old tree, how could you tell which were the dry years when the plant grew very little, and which were the wet years when the tree grew a lot?

The carbon cycle and the water cycle

Plants use carbon dioxide and water to make food. Animals eat plants and return carbon dioxide and water to the air as they breathe. In this way, both substances move in biological cycles in nature. Very many human processes, such as burning fuels, also create carbon dioxide and water.

Water also evaporates from the sea and forms clouds, from which the water returns to the land and sea as rain. This is another great natural cycle. Nitrogen also circulates among living things. For more about its cycle and the carbon cycle, see page 13 of 'What is food?"

The water cycle. Water is taken from the sea by evaporation and falls to the earth again as rain. Animals and plants need some of this water to live, but they also lose water into the atmosphere. Thus water is moving through the air and through living things in a continuous cycle ▼

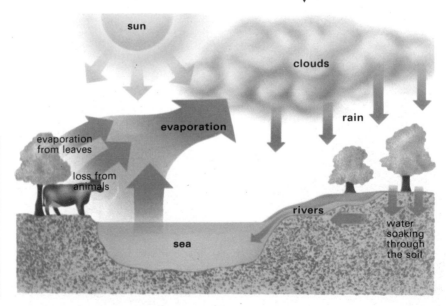

sun

clouds

evaporation

rain

evaporation from leaves

loss from animals

rivers

water soaking through the soil

sea

Too much and too little water

Instead of spring, summer, autumn and winter with some rain all the year round, some parts of the world have wet seasons and dry seasons. In this sort of climate, the land is usually very wet or very dry. The plants and animals here must be able to survive in these conditions.

Too much water

Water moves through plants, carrying salts to the leaves. If a plant lives in a very wet place it loses very little water through evaporation. If the water is not taken from the leaves, the plant has no need to suck more water from the ground. However, this would mean that the mineral salts were not being carried continuously to the leaves and the plant might die.

Plants which live in wet places must force water out of their leaves to make sure that water and minerals can still be sucked out of the ground. When water is forced out of a leaf, the leaf dies and falls off the plant.

Too little water

There are several reasons why a plant may not get enough water. There may not be enough rain, or the water around it may be too salty for it. In very cold places, all the water may be frozen solid. Plants which have adapted to living in dry places are called *xerophytes*.

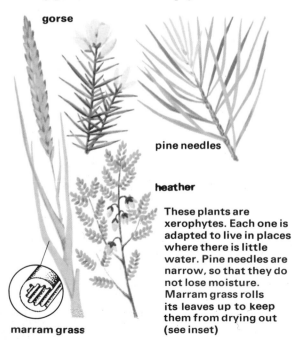

gorse

pine needles

heather

These plants are xerophytes. Each one is adapted to live in places where there is little water. Pine needles are narrow, so that they do not lose moisture. Marram grass rolls its leaves up to keep them from drying out (see inset)

marram grass

Sometimes the part of a desert plant above the ground dies. As soon as there is a rain storm the plant springs into life, sending leaves and flowers above the ground. Once it has rained many seeds which were lying dormant in the dry soil also spring into life, so for a short time the desert is a mass of colourful flowers

Desert plants must also be able to store water. Cacti store water in their stems. The giant saguaro cactus can take in over a tonne of water in a rainstorm

Desert temperatures vary from very hot to very cold. It can be as high as 55°C at midday in the Sahara, and drop to freezing at night.

As well as having to live with these temperature changes, plants must also be able to survive sand storms and occasional violent rainstorms. When rain does fall, it washes quickly through the sandy soil. Any minerals in the soil are washed away. In some places the soil is so poor and dry that nothing can live there.

Oases

When rain falls it sometimes runs into deep hollows. They are at least partly sheltered from the sun and so the water in them evaporates slowly. In the Sahara, these desert waterholes are called oases. Date palms and other plants with long roots can live at an oasis.

Desert animals

There are many desert animals. Some eat plants, some are hunters that eat other animals.

The best known desert animal is the camel. It is a large, plant-eating mammal which is used in Asia and the Middle East as a beast of burden.

The camel has broad soft feet which make it possible for the animal to walk across soft sand without sinking into it.

The camel can go for a long time without drinking but it cannot live without water altogether.

The camel's hump is made of fat. The camel uses this fat to provide energy. It can also break down the fat in its body to make water. The fat in the camel's hump can be used to make about 35 litres of water

Other animals lose water from their bodies when they sweat, and when they pass urine. The camel does not sweat. Instead, it lets its body temperature rise in the day time. It can cool off in the cold desert night. The camel's kidneys produce very little urine, and what there is, is very concentrated. This is because the camel takes most of the water from the urine back into its body.

Burrowing animals

Many desert animals burrow to escape the heat of the sun. This means they do not lose much water. They come out at night when it is cooler and safer than during the day. Many mammals burrow, and so do lizards, frogs and toads.

Finding water

If an animal fails to find water it will die. Vultures and other birds of prey flying above the desert can see a dying animal and swoop down to eat it. These birds get all the water they need from the animals they eat.

Flesh-eating mammals (*carnivores*) are not very good at saving water, and they cannot stay alive in the open desert. Most carnivores live near waterholes and wait for animals to come to drink. This way they can catch their food without having to go too far into the open desert.

Other animals, such as the desert tortoise, get the water they need from the plants they eat.

In forests, one animal out of 16 burrows

In grassland, 4 animals out of 16 burrow

One of the best ways of surviving in the hot desert is to find somewhere cool to hide during the day and to come out to look for food at night. For this reason, many animals in the desert burrow

In the desert, 12 animals out of 16 burrow

0 1 2 3 4 5 6 7 8 9 10 11 12 13 14 15 16

Many animals, like this Abert squirrel, solve the problem of surviving in a drought by hibernating in the driest seasons. During this time they neither eat, drink nor move about

1. Golden hamsters are popular pets even though they sleep most of the day. What advantage does being active at night give the hamster?
2. Why are insects with a thick skin or cuticle well adapted to living in the desert?
3. General Montgomery's Eighth Army called themselves the desert rats. Why do you think they chose this name?
4. Rattlesnakes do not drink. How do you think they get the water they need?

Digestion

Food is necessary to build up the body and to provide energy. Digestion is the process of taking food into the cells of the body. Digestion takes place all along the alimentary canal, the long tube which runs from the mouth to the anus.

Saliva

When we eat, the liquid in our mouths turns the food into a soft mash which is easy to swallow. The food is also mixed with enzymes while it is in the mouth, and these start to break it down. The liquid in the mouth, which contains these enzymes is called *saliva*. It is produced by the salivary glands.

Starch and glucose

Starch is one of the foods that provides energy. The main food substance in potatoes is starch. If you look at a potato cell through a microscope you will see the starch as small solid grains.

Starch and many other foods have large chemical molecules which are broken down into small molecules during digestion. This begins in the mouth where chewed-up food is mixed with saliva, which contains an enzyme that breaks starchy foods down. Starch is broken down in the body to glucose, which provides energy.

Athletes sometimes eat glucose tablets before a race, and people who are ill are given glucose drinks. A glucose meal provides energy much faster than one of bread and potatoes.

There is one salivary gland on each side of the mouth and one under the tongue. The saliva contains enzymes which start breaking the food down, and also make the food damp enough to taste and to be swallowed

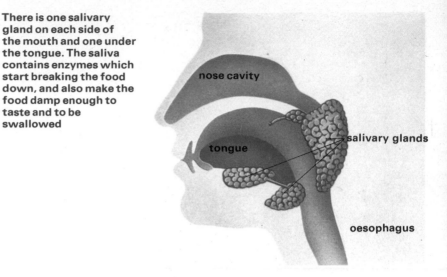

nose cavity

tongue

salivary glands

oesophagus

The stomach and small intestine

Other foods containing fats and proteins are mostly broken down in the stomach and intestine, by stomach acid and various enzymes. In the small intestine, bile from the gall bladder breaks down fats into very small droplets that can be absorbed into the body. Most of these broken-down foods are absorbed in the small intestine through tiny finger-like projections called *villi*. A few substances, however, including sugars and alcohol, are absorbed through the wall of the stomach into the bloodstream.

Lymph

Inside the villi are blood vessels and lymph vessels which carry the food substances away to all cells in the body. Lymph is a watery liquid which runs in tube-like vessels throughout the body. They join at various places with the blood vessels.

Many athletes take tablets of glucose to give them extra energy. Glucose is absorbed into the blood very quickly, and therefore gives energy fast

How food molecules enter the cell

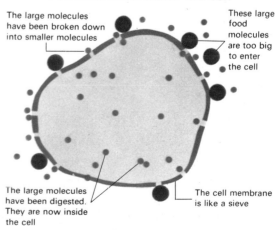

The large molecules have been broken down into smaller molecules

These large food molecules are too big to enter the cell

The large molecules have been digested. They are now inside the cell

The cell membrane is like a sieve

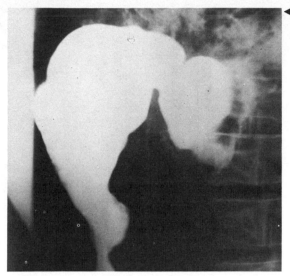

◄ An X-ray of the stomach containing barium. Barium is a metal which can be detected by X-rays when it is in the body. If a person is given a 'barium swallow', that is, if there is barium in their food, the progress of the food through the gut can be followed with X-rays. This shows how long the food stays in each part of the gut

The organs of digestion

The large intestine

The water in the alimentary canal is very valuable to the body and is re-absorbed in the large intestine. If something prevents the water being re-absorbed in this way then the result is diarrhoea. This usually only lasts for a few days but sometimes it can go on for much longer. If, for example, a person has cholera, a disease caused by bacteria, they can lose so much water in this way that they die.

When most of the water has been re-absorbed, the undigested food is kept in the rectum. It is expelled at regular intervals through the anus. Food is pushed through the alimentary canal from the mouth to the anus by the action of muscles. This is called *peristalsis*.

The liver

Harmful chemicals which get into the blood are made harmless by the liver (see pages 22 and 23). The liver also stores sugary, or carbohydrate, foods in the form of animal starch, or glycogen. When lots of energy is needed, as when exercising hard, the body draws on this stored energy.

Besides these foods, and water, the body needs small amounts of a number of vitamins and minerals. We do not usually have to worry about getting these because they are present in a normal diet. For more about this, see 'What is food?' in this series.

The liver ►
When a person has more sugary substances in his body than he needs, his liver stores the extra sugar. To do so it changes the sugar into glycogen. The liver is also the main organ of the body that removes poisons and makes them harmless

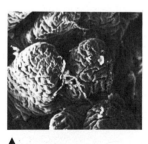

▲
The villi greatly magnified. Foods, already broken down in the stomach and intestine, pass into the villi. Inside each villus are blood and lymph vessels which take the food substances to all parts of the body

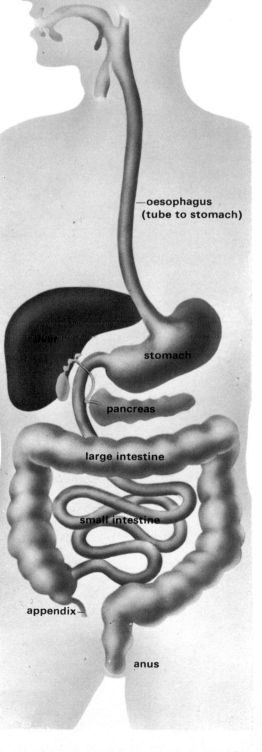

—oesophagus (tube to stomach)

liver

stomach

pancreas

large intestine

small intestine

appendix—

anus

1. Why do foods taste less appetising when they are dry than when they are soaked and cooked?
2. Why is it important to give people who have 'upset stomachs' a lot of liquid to drink?
3. How do digested fats eventually enter the blood?

Blood

The blood is the body's transport system. It is pumped around the body by the heart. The main blood vessels are the *veins* and *arteries*. They carry all digested food, oxygen, carbon dioxide, hormones, wastes and heat around the body.

The arteries branch out into fine tubes called *capillaries*. These run between the cells to provide them with essential chemicals, and to remove waste chemicals. The capillaries join up again to form the veins, which lead back to the heart. The blood is kept flowing in the correct direction by a system of *valves*.

Blood is pumped under pressure so it is very important that the veins are strong and can change shape as the body moves. If the walls of the veins become weak, the veins swell. This swelling puts extra pressure on the valves causing *varicose veins* in the main veins.

Plasma

Blood is red because it contains red blood cells called *corpuscles*. It also contains colourless cells called white cells. The red and white cells float in a straw-coloured liquid called *plasma*. This liquid is mainly water. It gets its colour from chemicals which are dissolved in it.

Plasma carries digested food to the liver and then to the cells of the body. It carries waste from the liver to the kidneys. It takes salts to the skin (these are what make sweat taste salty). The chemicals which control growth, sexual development and all sorts of other activities are carried dissolved in the plasma.

The plasma is so important that after an accident, if someone is losing a lot of blood, it is often more important to replace the liquid plasma than the blood complete with cells.

The circulation of the blood

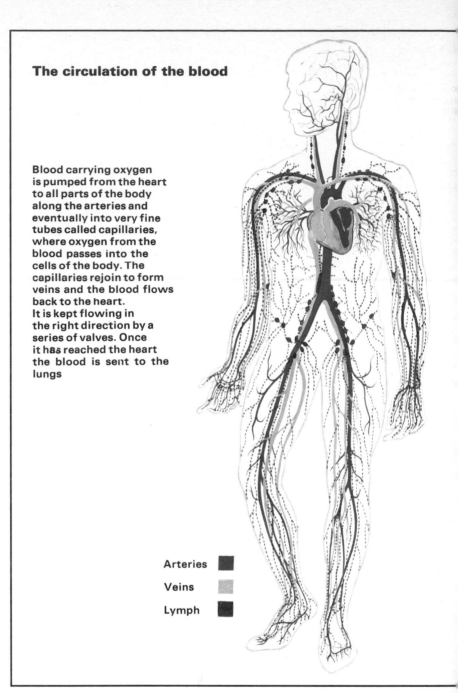

Blood carrying oxygen is pumped from the heart to all parts of the body along the arteries and eventually into very fine tubes called capillaries, where oxygen from the blood passes into the cells of the body. The capillaries rejoin to form veins and the blood flows back to the heart. It is kept flowing in the right direction by a series of valves. Once it has reached the heart the blood is sent to the lungs

Arteries ▢

Veins ▢

Lymph ▢

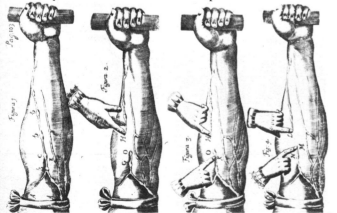

◀ William Harvey, a seventeenth century doctor, did experiments to test how much blood was pumped from the heart in one hour. The experiments led him to realise that blood circulates around the body.
Far left. Part of the record of his experiments

1. Which is the tissue in the body which has the most water in it?
2. Find out your pulse rate per minute. Run up and down on the spot for one minute, and count your pulse rate again. Work out how much faster it is then.
3. Why is the heart muscle on the left-hand side of the

18

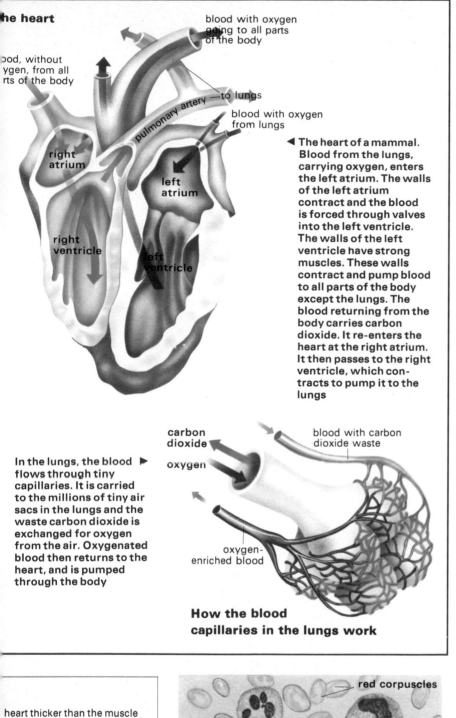

he heart

blood with oxygen going to all parts of the body

ood, without ygen, from all rts of the body

pulmonary artery —to lungs

blood with oxygen from lungs

right atrium

left atrium

right ventricle

left ventricle

◀ **The heart of a mammal. Blood from the lungs, carrying oxygen, enters the left atrium. The walls of the left atrium contract and the blood is forced through valves into the left ventricle. The walls of the left ventricle have strong muscles. These walls contract and pump blood to all parts of the body except the lungs. The blood returning from the body carries carbon dioxide. It re-enters the heart at the right atrium. It then passes to the right ventricle, which contracts to pump it to the lungs**

carbon dioxide

oxygen

blood with carbon dioxide waste

oxygen-enriched blood

In the lungs, the blood ▶ flows through tiny capillaries. It is carried to the millions of tiny air sacs in the lungs and the waste carbon dioxide is exchanged for oxygen from the air. Oxygenated blood then returns to the heart, and is pumped through the body

How the blood capillaries in the lungs work

heart thicker than the muscle on the right-hand side?
4. Make a list of the main differences between arteries and veins and capillaries. Find out and explain the meanings of the following words: tourniquet, transfusion, pacemaker, stethoscope and electrocardiogram.

red corpuscles

Red and white blood cells. The blood also contains platelets, which are very tiny. They play an important part in the clotting process

white cells

Red blood cells

Oxygen from the lungs enters the red cells and joins the chemical in them which is called *haemoglobin*. This chemical is red and gives the blood its colour. This combination of oxygen and haemoglobin (*oxyhaemoglobin*) gives away the oxygen in the capillaries to cells, particularly working muscles. The oxygen is still dissolved in water and it goes to cells where it is used in energy production. Unlike other cells, red cells lose their *controlling nucleus*. This is why they are called corpuscles and not cells. These red corpuscles are replaced continuously by the red bone marrow. If a person loses blood, the marrow soon replaces red corpuscles, but there must be enough liquid plasma for them.

In each species of animal, the red blood corpuscles are more or less the same as each other. But the white cells are different sizes from one another, and all help to protect the body in different ways.

For example, when harmful bacteria get into a cut or scratch, some types of white blood cells attach themselves to the bacteria before they can multiply and spread. The result is *pus*, which is a mixture of dead body cells which have been destroyed by the bacteria, living white cells, bacteria killed by the white cells and any surviving bacteria. Some white cells engulf bacteria, others destroy them.

The plasma carries special substances which form a net over a cut to keep the blood in. Red blood corpuscles are caught in the net, forming a protective scab over the cut. When the damage has been repaired the scab falls off. Vitamin K plus blood *platelets* have to be present before blood will clot.

Sometimes a blood clot forms inside the body. It can travel inside the arteries. If a clot touches the brain or heart it can cause paralysis and can even be fatal.

Some people suffer from a condition called haemophilia, which means their blood does not clot. If they cut themselves, even slightly, they can bleed to death. Some of Queen Victoria's descendants suffered from this. One of them was the son of Tsar Nicholas II, the last Tsar of Russia

19

Keeping cool

As the body heats up, the sweat glands become more active. Sweat glands are coiled tubes under the skin in which water collects and then escapes to the surface of the skin through the sweat *pores*.

The evaporation of sweat takes heat from the skin, which in turn takes heat from the blood in the capillaries. This cools the body down. If the body does not sweat, the temperature will rise. It cannot rise too far without causing damage.

If the weather is humid and 'sticky', water cannot evaporate very quickly from the skin. This makes us feel very uncomfortable and sweaty, and there is even a danger of overheating. A covering of something waterproof, like paint, would make a person overheat in the same way. Anti-perspirants and deodorants reduce sweating, and they should only be used on a small part of the body at one time.

If you put a little methylated spirits on the back of your hand, and then blow on it, the spirits will evaporate. Your skin will feel cool because the evaporating liquid takes heat from your hand. Perfumes and after shave lotions work in the same way, and so they too feel cool.

Children in New York keep cool by playing under a fire hydrant

A sweat gland. Although ▶ sweat is always present it is only noticeable when it reaches the surface of the skin

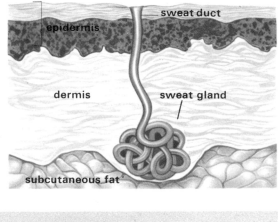

epidermis

sweat duct

dermis

sweat gland

subcutaneous fat

Sweating

Most mammals have a more or less constant body temperature. The average body temperature of a human is usually 37°C (98·4°F). If the body temperature is any higher it probably means that the person has been working very hard or that they are ill.

If the body gets overheated, it must be able to cool down.

The human body cools through evaporation. You sweat and the sweat evaporates. This cools you down. Sweat is mainly water, and though it does not evaporate as fast as methylated spirits or perfume (and therefore does not feel quite as cool) it is still useful for cooling the body.

Other mammals sweat too. Both cattle and horses sweat. A horse can cool itself down until it gets too cold, so that after a race when the horse has been sweating a lot, it should be covered with a blanket to keep it warm.

As the body heats up, the blood vessels near the surface of the skin get slightly wider. More blood flows through the vessels, so that it is better cooled by the air. The increased blood flow makes the skin look red.

A horse sweating after a race. It should be covered with a blanket to prevent it from cooling down so much that it begins to suffer

When a dog pants, moisture evaporates from its tongue. This causes heat to be lost, so cooling the dog's body ◀

▶ Like the children in New York, this elephant is keeping cool by taking a shower

Hippos wallowing in the water. They spend much of the day (nearly half) submerged in this way, keeping cool. At night they come out on to land and look for food ▼

Panting

Mammals, such as dogs, which have thick coats, have very few sweat glands. When a dog is hot, it *pants*. Panting is heavy breathing with the tongue hanging out. The dog loses water by evaporating it from its mouth and lungs, and this helps to cool the animal down.

Other ways of keeping cool

Elephants can cool themselves by spraying water all over their bodies with their trunks. When they are away from water, the hot sun warms the elephants up again. They have other ways of keeping cool, for example, by flapping their enormous ears. The blood capillaries in their ears lose heat to the surrounding air.

The hippopotamus, the elephant and the water buffalo like to wade in soft, wet mud. The mud is cool to wallow in, and, for some time after the animal has left the mud, it is kept cool by water evaporating from the coating of mud on its body.

Mud also gives protection from insect bites. When it has dried out the animal is the same colour as the earth around it. This makes it difficult for its enemies to see it, so that the mud also works as a camouflage.

1. Why do athletes put track suits on immediately after a race?
2. Why do people go red in the face after they have been running fast?
3. Jerboas are small rodents that live in the desert. They only come out of their burrows at night. Why do you think this is so?
4. Why do dogs moult?

Elephants wallowing in the mud

Removing waste products

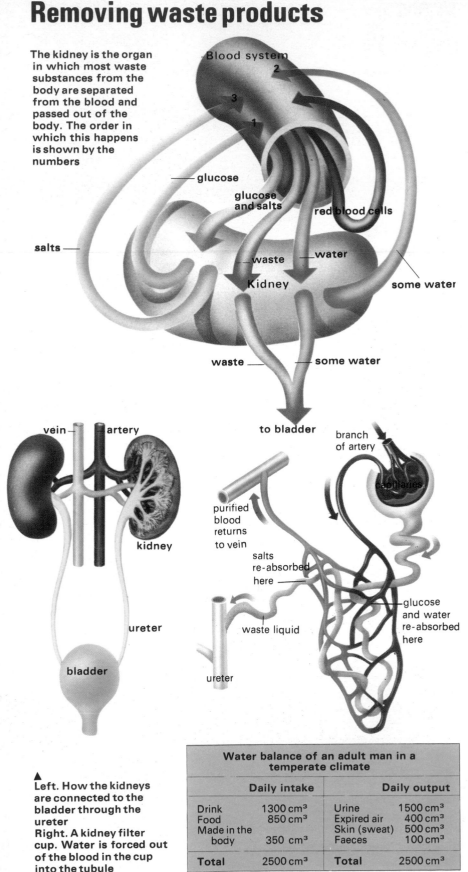

The kidney is the organ in which most waste substances from the body are separated from the blood and passed out of the body. The order in which this happens is shown by the numbers

Blood system
glucose
glucose and salts
red blood cells
salts
waste
water
Kidney
some water
waste
some water
to bladder

branch of artery
vein
artery
capillaries
purified blood returns to vein
kidney
salts re-absorbed here
glucose and water re-absorbed here
waste liquid
ureter
ureter
bladder

▲ Left. How the kidneys are connected to the bladder through the ureter
Right. A kidney filter cup. Water is forced out of the blood in the cup into the tubule

Water balance of an adult man in a temperate climate			
Daily intake		**Daily output**	
Drink	1300 cm³	Urine	1500 cm³
Food	850 cm³	Expired air	400 cm³
Made in the body	350 cm³	Skin (sweat)	500 cm³
		Faeces	100 cm³
Total	**2500 cm³**	**Total**	**2500 cm³**

All the cells in our bodies need oxygen and food, and produce waste. Some of the chemicals in the waste are poisonous, and the body must get rid of them.

One of the wastes is carbon dioxide, which is carried by the blood to the lungs and lost when we breathe out. Other wastes, called nitrogenous wastes because they contain nitrogen, are carried by the blood to the liver where they are changed into a less harmful substance called *urea*. The urea is then carried in the blood to the kidneys.

The kidneys

A mammal has two kidneys. These are at the back of the body, just above the waist. The *renal* artery brings the blood which is carrying the urea to the kidneys.

The urea is separated from the blood in the kidney. The blood then leaves the kidney through the renal vein. The waste substances run down from the kidneys through two tubes called *ureters*. There is one ureter from each kidney. They run down into the bladder, where the waste is stored until it is passed out of the body.

The inner part of the kidney is mainly a mass of tubes. It has an outer layer or *cortex*, where the waste is filtered from the blood. There are about one million cup-shaped filters in the cortex of each kidney. There are very small blood vessels or capillaries in each cup. These are so fine that as the heart forces blood through them, the water in the plasma is forced out into the tubes. Urea and many other chemicals are dissolved in the water. They too are taken from the blood. The useful chemicals, such as glucose, water and salts, are taken back into the blood. The rest is waste. For more about excretion, see 'What happens to food' pages 20/21.

Water balance

By the time the waste liquid reaches the tube to the bladder, everything in the waste which is useful to the body has been re-absorbed into the bloodstream. Urine is mainly urea dissolved in water. The body produces about one and a half litres of urine a day, though the amount changes from day to day.

The quantity of water the body loses each day is the same as the quantity taken in. A person who drinks a lot of liquid, will pass a lot of urine. A person who sweats a lot will pass less urine than they would if they were losing water through urine alone. The table on the left gives an example of water balance.

Transplants and machines

If a kidney is damaged by disease or through an accident, it cannot remove the waste urea. If both kidneys are damaged, the level of poisonous urea in the body rises, and the person will probably die.

There are two ways of saving a person whose kidneys do not work. The first is to replace a damaged kidney with another, through a *transplant* operation.

The second method is to pass a patient's blood through a *kidney machine*. This machine can clean the blood in the way the kidneys themselves do, but the machine is expensive and awkward to use. Transplanting is a better solution, but it does not always work because the patient's body may reject the new kidney.

Producing less watery waste

Animals need a certain amount of water every day just to carry away the urea which is produced by the breakdown of cells. In humans this amount is about a litre.

Animals which drink very little must produce waste chemicals which are not poisonous, and which can leave the body without losing too much water.

Grasshoppers and locusts change their waste into nitrogenous crystals (crystals containing nitrogen). These are crystals of *uric acid*. Solid crystals cannot move through the body very easily, and this movement would hurt the grasshopper. To prevent this, the crystals go straight into the alimentary canal. They pass through the body with the waste food.

Insects are not the only creatures which live in dry places. Many snakes and lizards live in rocky areas where there is not much water. Like the grasshopper, they produce solid uric acid.

Birds produce this acid as well. Bird lime, or *guano*, is uric acid made by the bird's kidneys. Most of the water from the waste is taken back into the bird's body. This leaves a white paste. You can see this on buildings where pigeons have been roosting.

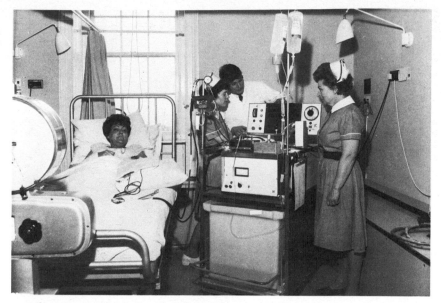

A kidney machine. This machine acts as an artificial kidney when a person's kidneys are not working properly. The machine contains long lengths of visking tubing, submerged in various liquids. As the blood flows through the tubes, wastes pass through the tube into the liquids. The blood is purified and can be passed back into the body. This treatment has to be repeated every two or three days, or the patient is made very ill by the wastes in her blood

Fish and osmosis

Sea water contains a solution of salt. The process called osmosis (see page 9) means that any less dense water which is in the living things in the sea could be drawn out by the sea water.

If a fresh-water fish were placed in sea water, it would lose water by osmosis and die. But fish like sharks which live in the sea can prevent water loss. They too use the process of osmosis. Their livers make urea, but instead of having it removed by the kidneys at once, some of the urea is stored in the bloodstream. This means that the solution inside the fish is stronger than the solution in the sea water.

The fish needs 2 per cent to 2·5 per cent of urea in its blood to make the solution strong enough to stop water being drawn into the sea.

Although 2 per cent does not seem much urea for an animal to store in its body, less than one tenth of this would kill most animals.

1. Name two ways in which the body keeps its water content at the right level. What is dehydration?
2. Find out about diabetes and why people who suffer from diabetes have special food containing artificial sweeteners.
3. Why do insects produce uric acid rather than urea? What would be the disadvantages of our liver producing uric acid instead of urea?

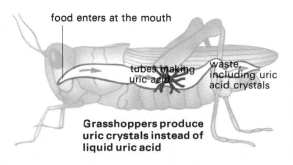

food enters at the mouth

tubes making uric acid

waste, including uric acid crystals

Grasshoppers produce uric crystals instead of liquid uric acid

Freshwater animals usually cannot live in the sea, and vice versa. But, salmon live part of their life in fresh water and part in the sea. Such animals have to develop special means of coping with these 'osmotic' changes

Man and water

Water is used to a large extent in generating electricity. The machinery used gets very hot and has to be cooled by water. The water is then cooled down in giant cooling towers

A pumping station. Water is being pumped from a river. It will be purified and then sent to people's houses as tap water

Drinking in space. Liquid has to be contained securely, otherwise, with no gravity to hold it in one place, it would simply fly about the spacecraft

Some of the water used in the home	
The body needs: **1·5 litres**	A small washing machine uses: **35 litres**
Flushing a toilet: **9 litres**	A shallow bath: **70 litres**

The human body, like the bodies of other animals, is mainly made up of water. We drink water, and we take it in with our food. A person needs to drink about 1·5 litres of water a day, but we use a lot more water for other things. For example, water is used to prepare vegetables, wash up, and washing of all kinds.

Using water in industry

Vast quantities of water are used in industry. Over 200 000 litres of water are used to make the steel for one large car. Another 36 000 litres are used while the car is being assembled. More still is used to make the tyres, windows, seats, and so on, and 170 litres was used for every bag of cement that was used to make the factory.

Recycling water

Water returns to the air through evaporation in the water cycle. But this natural cycle is too slow for people to rely on. In many large towns, water has to be taken from nearby rivers, purified, used, and then returned from the sewage farms to the river.

Further along the river another town may use the river water, so that the same water may be used several times before it reaches the sea.

Astronauts and water

When astronauts go into space, they must be supplied with air, food, water and ways of disposing of their wastes. Space journeys so far have been short, and astronauts have been able to carry enough water in the spacecraft. But on longer journeys this is not possible and space travellers on longer trips have to use a system of recycling water.

1. Wash your hands under a running tap, and collect the water used while you did this. Compare this with the amount of water you would use if you washed your hands in a bowl of water. Which method saves water? How much?
2. Find out where the water in your taps come from, where and how it is purified, and where it goes after use.